More *Than* Forgiven

MORE
THAN
FORGIVEN

*Freedom, Identity, and Rest
Through Union With Jesus*

RENÉE H. BERRY

HIGH BRIDGE
BOOKS & MEDIA

More than Forgiven
by Renée H. Berry

Copyright © 2026

All rights reserved.

Printed in the United States of America

ISBN: 978-1-962802-75-8

High Bridge Books titles may be purchased in bulk for educational, business, fundraising, or sales promotional use. For information, please contact High Bridge Books via www.HighBridgeBooks.com/contact. Published in Houston, Texas, by High Bridge Books.

MORE THAN FORGIVEN is a powerful book that speaks from the heart of God's Scriptural truth to the heart of every person desiring to walk in greater intimacy with Him. Each entry guides the reader toward an experiential and practical understanding of the grace and freedom God offers to all who believe. In many ways, it is a breath of fresh air and a relief from the striving and fear that drive many believers.

> — **PAT GRAHAM**, Former President and Co-founder of Abundant Grace International

MORE THAN FORGIVEN would be an excellent gift to be given to encourage: a new believer, a discipleship class, a companion resource for individual discipleship counseling, or for your own spiritual maturity in Christ. We found that reading through the entries in this book, with New Covenant scriptures and thought-provoking questions, strengthened us in our ongoing spiritual journey, pointing us to revelation Truth. Lies are exposed by Christ, so that we can walk free of defeating thought patterns as He works in us to will and do His good pleasure. This writing reveals the beautiful Truth of who God says we are, Who He says He is, and how much we are dearly loved.

> — **JOE AND JEAN NESBITT** - former directors of Grace Life International, Asheville, NC

"God, are You enough?" That question rocked my world the first morning I read it in **MORE THAN FORGIVEN**. The answer was an easy, "Yes" in my head, but my heart? Not quite. Even though I have been teaching Christ as Life for over 27 years, I had to be honest with myself. I haven't always applied to my own self what I've taught others. With family, ministry, health, and personal issues challenging me, that question caught me trying to live out of my own resources and smarts.

This book pulls the cover off the "I got this" mentality and reveals that it is He, not us, Who works, loves, heals, fixes, and transforms. What a relief!! What is our role? Believe, trust, and let Him! What a healing tool Renée Berry and **MORE THAN FORGIVEN** are in His hands.

> — **DR. PAUL CREWS**, Elder, More2Life Ministries; Director, Great Exchange Ministries, Okeechobee, FL

DEDICATION

To those who tirelessly counsel, teach, pastor, and mentor the truths of the New Covenant—callings that are not for the faint of heart.

Thank you to my editor, D'Etta Lasky, for the countless hours she worked tirelessly to make this manuscript what it is! Her expert formatting and incredible understanding of the New Covenant enriched every aspect of this book. I am so grateful, De!

I am always grateful to those whom God has chosen for me to walk with in like-mindedness in this life. Jean Nesbitt, Velda Jones, and Pat Graham spent hours with me, putting in the finishing touches to the manuscript, ensuring that the entries gave credence to the Truths of the New Covenant and that the Scriptures lined up with each lesson. I'm eternally grateful, Sisters!

My old identity has been co-crucified with Christ and no longer lives. And now the essence of this new life is no longer mine, for the Anointed One lives his life through me—we live in union as one! My new life is empowered by the faith of the Son of God who loves me so much that he gave himself for me, dispensing his life into mine!

— (Galatians 2:20, TPT)

CONTENTS

FOREWORD

Welcome to **MORE THAN FORGIVEN**. This study is designed to introduce you to, and guide you through, the truth of living the New Covenant life through moment-by-moment dependence on Christ. You will be led into a clear, Scriptural understanding of your union with Him, empowering you to live from His very nature, attributes, and characteristics as you trust Him for the new life He secured for you at the cross. What a beautiful journey it is to discover the depths of who God is and your true identity in union with Him!

Intimacy with the Trinity is the goal. This study will help you remove the blocks that try to keep you from the Abundant Life that is yours in Christ. It is exciting to witness Jesus breaking through places in your soul that you consider impossible to heal. Indeed, nothing is impossible with God. As the Lord deals with such areas, His responsibility is to heal, sanctify, and hallow you with His Life being lived through you as you. Your responsibility is to believe and receive the finished work of the cross done on your behalf.

Enjoy the journey!

Introduction

OUR UNDERSTANDING OF THE SANCTIFICATION journey is to accept that God is making real in our soul (mind, will, and emotions) through experience what He has already accomplished in our spirit through the finished work of the cross and our union with Christ. Christ is the focus – not us. The looming question that sends us on our quest and is embodied in every mind (whether we are conscious of it or not) is, "God, are You enough?" A fleshly response is, "No!" Adam and Eve incorrectly answered that question for us in the Garden, and we, when responding in our flesh (our way of meeting our needs apart from total dependence on Jesus Christ), answer it the same way until we are healed (Genesis 3:1-8; Isaiah 30:18-22; Jeremiah 30:12-18).

Our "Truth" as Christians is not a concept but a Person—Jesus Christ (John 14:6). In John 6:28–29, Jesus makes clear that the work God requires of us can be summed up in one word: *believe*. Believe in Jesus, whom God has sent. Believe who Jesus reveals God to be, and believe who Jesus reveals us to be. All Truth resides in Christ alone and is unveiled to us through the Holy Spirit. Through the cross, the gap between God and humanity was permanently closed, securing an intimate relationship with a loving God. God's original purpose for humanity—union with Himself through Christ—was never lost. The focus has always been on God, not on us.

Today, with our spirits sealed in Christ by the Holy Spirit, we live in union with Christ and can embrace the New Covenant—a Covenant of love, grace, mercy, and life (2 Corinthians 1:22; Ephesians 1:13). All we are commanded to do is believe who Jesus is as revealed to us by the Holy Spirit. This seems so simple until we encounter the Truth about the opposition we face in 1 John 2:15-16. Three primary foes constantly war against us: the world, the flesh, and the devil. These are relentless foes that come at us every minute of every day. The erroneous thought arises, "If I mature or if I can grasp this Biblical principle, then life here will not be so hard!" This could be why so many Christians live defeated lives. They are trying to grasp the unattainable, victory in their strength by doing "something" they think will win the battle for themselves—impossible! Why? Because the victory is already won. God wants us to live from what He has accomplished and freely given us. That is, everything for life and godliness (2 Peter 1:3). The focus can never be on us. It must always be on Christ, the Hope of Glory.

God's unique plan for every believer was set before the foundation of the world (Jeremiah 29:11; Psalm 139:16). He carries out that plan through the circumstances of daily living (Romans 8:28). In those circumstances, we find our God-given needs for love, acceptance, worth, and security are met in Christ alone, not in anyone or anything else. As a result, He is making us and molding us into the image of Christ (Romans 8:29). LIFE, true LIFE, is in our Lord and Savior, Jesus Christ. The experience of His Life is through belief as we, by faith, not by sight, depend on Christ moment by moment, incident by incident, to be everything, our All in All and our Enough. He did not leave us here on this earth to live our lives independently. He designed us to depend totally on Him as He did with the Father (John 17). When we do not, we suffer because of the agreement we make with the lies of our flesh, the world, and the devil. As we believe those lies, we go our own way by trying to determine what might meet our needs or make us feel better.

Jesus told us in Luke 10:27 to love the Lord our God with all our heart, soul, strength, and mind, and our neighbors as ourselves. Satan began in the Garden of Eden with Adam and Eve to try to dissuade man from the Truth about God, ourselves, and others. His mission is to kill, steal from, and destroy us, a people designed by God for Life in Christ (John 10:10). It is essential to know the enemy's strategy against us. It is this strategy that keeps us from daily dependence on Christ. What will be revealed in these writings is not a formula for living the Christian life but a relationship and a focus on the only Person, Jesus Christ, who can deliver us from the lies of our flesh, the worldly thinking and ways, and the enemy. All Jesus asks us to do is believe—believe Who He says He is and believe who He says we are; from our union with Christ, our TRUE identity is in Him.

More than Enough

THIS SECTION CONTAINS 40 ENTRIES CONSISTING of the following:

THE TRUTH

Each day has a truth stating who you are in Christ or Who God is.

The Questions

After reading the entry, there are activation questions to study, journal, and pray over.

Scripture

Following each truth will be key Scriptures for further learning, reflection, and growth. As you read them, allow the Holy Spirit to minister to and heal you. It is the Truth of God that will set you free.

Appendix:

Some entries will have an appendix for further growth: journal personal revelation, study, prayers, activations, etc. These are found in the back of the book.

1

THE INDWELLING PRESENCE: LIFE WITH THE HOLY SPIRIT

THE TRUTH

I AM IN THE FULLNESS OF THE TRINITY—FATHER, Son, and Holy Spirit. I AM sent because Jesus went back to the Father. My still small voice, not found in the wind, the earthquake, or the fire, will speak to you. I, the Holy Spirit, will be your Comforter, Counselor, Helper, Advocate, Intercessor, Paraclete, Strengthener, and Standby. Listen to Me, not just for this moment, but for every moment you are on this earth. Listen! I illuminate the Scriptures. I invade your thoughts. I speak through others. I sing over you. I am in nature. Fine-tune your eyes and ears to Me. I, the Holy Spirit, am always with you.

The Questions

Do you believe the Trinity loves you unconditionally? How have you personally experienced that love and guidance into The Truth (beyond head knowledge)?

Scripture

John 17	John 14:23-26	John 10
1 Kings 19:11-12	John 16:7	Matthew 28:20
Zephaniah 3:17	Ephesians 3:19	Romans 1:19-20

> John 17:26…I will continue to make You (God) even more real to them, so that they may experience the same endless love that You have for me…

2

Turning to the Way: Salvation and New Life in Christ

THE TRUTH

I F YOU HAVE NOT YET RECEIVED CHRIST THE LORD as your Savior, then I AM here to convict you of your sin and your great need for a Savior. Your life needs to be saved for eternity. It would be best if you turned from your own way of figuring out your life. You were never meant to live apart from Me. Turn to Me (Jesus) to live by faith. I AM the Way, the Truth, and the Life. I want to mold and make you in My image. Come to Me as you are.

THE QUESTIONS

How do you feel about living life on your own? Why do you need Jesus to save (deliver) you?

SCRIPTURE

John 16:8-9	John 14:6	Ezekiel 36:26-27
Ephesians 2:1-5	2 Corinthians 5:17	John 3:16
Ephesians 2:8-9	John 1:12-13	

John 14:6 – I am the Way, the Truth, and the Life; no one comes to the Father except by (through) Me.

3

THE PLUMB LINE OF TRUTH: GOD'S WORD AS FINAL AUTHORITY

THE TRUTH

I AM THE GOD OF THE BIBLE. THE FIRST THING you must settle in your mind is to believe and receive the Scriptures as Truth—the plumb line by which you measure every thought, feeling, circumstance, relationship, and decision. Everything you need to know about Me, about yourself, and about others is revealed in the Scriptures by Me, the Holy Spirit. The world, the flesh, and the devil relentlessly contend for your mind, seeking to rob you of Truth. A battle rages within you—to live by the flesh or to walk by the Spirit. You overcome only as you depend fully on Christ as your Life. I will expose the lies that must be exchanged for the Truth of who I say I AM and who I say you are. As that Truth becomes your reality, you will walk in victory in Me, the Holy Spirit, moment by moment.

THE QUESTIONS

You have a choice: trusting Me to walk you through painful places to be set free, or not; which do you choose? What blocks your complete trust in me?

SCRIPTURE

Exodus 3:14   Romans 8:4-6 (TPT)
Isaiah 28:17 (TPT)   1 John 2:15-16 (AMPC)
John 6:28-29

John 6:28-29 - ...this is the work that God asks of you: that you believe in the One (Jesus) Whom He (the Father) has sent...

4

THE GREAT PHYSICIAN: HEALING THE WOUNDED HEART

THE TRUTH

TODAY'S CIRCUMSTANCES ARE NO ACCIDENT, not even the act of reading this entry. It is part of My plan for you to receive this message today and begin or continue your soul-healing process, which is your sanctification. Are you surprised to find out that your hurt is incurable, that nothing you have tried in your own strength binds your wound(s)? It is as if everything and everyone you have gone after to fill those places for love, acceptance, worth, and security has forgotten and abandoned you. Are you shocked to know that I say it was Me Who allowed these things to happen? I did it so you would know that nothing or no one fully meets your needs except Me. I am the only One Who can heal your wounded heart and your damaged emotions. That is My promise to you. "For I will restore health to you, and I will heal your wounds." I will carefully unbind the covering on the wounds so I can apply My healing plaster, My unconditional love, and Truth. It is the only thing that will heal and seal the wound forever. I AM your Great Physician.

THE QUESTIONS

By faith, do you believe only I can bring Truth and Freedom from the deep pain of the wounds? What might healing look like for you?

SCRIPTURE

Jeremiah 30:12-17   Jonah 2:8
Jeremiah 8:22 (AMPC)   Galatians 5:1 (AMPC)

Galatians 5:1 (TPT) – At last we have freedom, for Christ has set us free!

5

THE FIRST EXCHANGE: WHEN DEPENDENCE WAS LOST

THE TRUTH

ON OUR JOURNEY TOGETHER, WE MUST LOOK back at the Garden where it all began. When Adam and Eve were deceived, they fell into a pit of doubt, lies, and denial. The deception, instilled by the Evil One, led them to choose each other to fulfill their God-given needs for love, acceptance, worth, and security. The moment Eve bit the fruit from the Tree of the Knowledge of Good and Evil, she was changed. When Adam saw she was changed, he, too, bit the fruit, thus choosing another person, apart from God, as his all in all and his enough. I never intended for anyone to be a substitute for My relationship with you. Let Me show you if you have believed the lie that someone or something else can take the place of Me in your life to meet your God-given needs. I want to show you how to exchange that lie for the Truth. I am willing to shed Light on the lie.

The Questions

Will you let Me show you the root of the lie, the time you began to trust another to meet the needs only I can meet? What do you believe the lie to be that needs to be exchanged for the Truth?

Scripture

Genesis 3:1-8   John 14:6   Ephesians 5:8-9
Psalm139:23-24 (TPT)   Colossians 1:13

> Colossians 1:13 – For He rescued us from the domain of darkness, and transferred us to the kingdom of His beloved Son…

6

The Death of the Human Spirit: How Shame Entered the Soul

THE TRUTH

As a result of the fall, I promised Adam and Eve they would die. They did not die a physical death. What died, you may ask? Their human spirit died. They broke their relationship and fellowship with Me to become the god of their own life. They were no longer spirit to Spirit with Me. As a result, they also became their own judge. What I had spoken as good (naked and vulnerable), they now saw as shameful and deemed themselves unacceptable. So, they covered up. They hid from Me, an intimate God, Who had given them everything for an abundant life. They were fearful and saw Me as angry, as a God who would come after them and judge them. They exchanged their lens of Love for the enemy's lens of fear. They now believed they could get their God-given needs for love, acceptance, worth, and security met in and through each other; that is relational idolatry (codependency). No longer would they depend on Me to meet those needs. Your love lens has become distorted, too, due to the Fall. When you choose to look at life through circumstances and relationships, the truth about Me, yourself, and others becomes distorted. I can untwist that for you with the Truth, but you must be willing to be naked and vulnerable.

THE QUESTIONS

What are the sources from which you try to derive life (i.e., a relationship, spouse, children, job, money, success, etc.)? Are you willing to come to Me and confess that so you can exchange the lie for the Truth and agree with it?

SCRIPTURE

Genesis 3:1-13   Isaiah 53:6
John 14:6   2 Peter 1:3

> Genesis 3:4 – But the serpent said to the woman,
> You shall not surely die…

7

Idols Exposed: Learning to Depend on God Alone

THE TRUTH

I SET A PLAN FOR YOUR LIFE BEFORE THE foundation of the world. The healing of your heart will come as you see you cannot live the plan in your own strength. You were never meant to analyze your life and logically figure out what you will do. Trust Me to bring you to the place where you'll see your desperate need for Me. Nothing and no one else will suffice. I want all your idols—those things you are depending on for life and to meet your God-given needs instead of Me. It is My job to show you what those idols are. Trust Me to give you the desire to come to Me. I will remove the idols as you surrender them to Me. Then, and only then, do I become Life to you.

THE QUESTION

What/who do you depend on to meet your God-given needs for love, acceptance, worth, and security apart from total dependence on Me?

SCRIPTURE

Ephesians 3:1-15	Jonah 2:8	John 14:6
Jeremiah 29:11	Isaiah 27:9	1 Thessalonians 1:9-10
Isaiah 30:18-22	Romans 5:10	

1 Thessalonians 1:9 - ...everyone knows how wonderfully you turned to God from idols to serve the true and living God...

8

A New Identity: Learning to Live From Righteousness, Not Sin

THE TRUTH

WHEN YOU HAVE A SAVING RELATIONSHIP with the Lord Jesus (faith in Him, alone, to save you with His Eternal Life), I will constantly and consistently remind you of who you are and Whose you are. You have a new heart and a new spirit. Therefore, you have a new nature, Christ's nature. You are no longer identified by sin but by the righteousness of God in Christ Jesus. I will never again directly point to your sin. I will only remind you of your righteousness and who you are in Christ. I will point to your new identity. If you become entangled in sin, I will first show you your true identity of righteousness and holiness. From that vantage point, you will see you are not living out of your union with Christ. You can choose to continue to walk according to your flesh, or you can choose the Spirit, therefore, living out of your identity in Christ, the

real you. Because you are now identified with Me, you have My nature, My attributes, and My characteristics. I will renew your mind to the Truth—believe and receive!

The Question

Do you judge and define yourself by your behavior? How could believing that Jesus crucified your old man with his sinful nature and resurrected you in union with Himself, therefore, with His nature, change your behavior?

Scripture

Romans 12:2	Ezekiel 36:26-27	Jeremiah 31:34
Hebrews 8:12	John 6:28-29	Romans 5
Romans 6	Romans 8:1	Galatians 2:20 (TPT)

Hebrews 8:12 - ...(I will) never remember again their sins...

9

RECOGNIZING THE ENEMY'S VOICE

THE TRUTH

DO YOU HEAR A VOICE TELLING YOU THAT you are no good, unacceptable, or better than everyone else? Does that same voice tell you that God is untrustworthy, unloving, uncaring, or just a grandpa in the sky? What about the voice that tells you not to trust others or let them get close to you? That is not your voice speaking to you. It is the voice of the enemy who can make his voice sound like yours. Ask yourself, "Would Jesus ever speak to me like that?" The healing of your heart from past hurts and rejections that came through relationships and circumstances will enable you to hear My voice clearly. Let me show you those past hurts and what you believed. They are a block to The Way—the Abundant Life Jesus promised you while here on earth.

The Questions

Can you identify the lies you agree with being whispered in your ear that place doubt in you about God, self, and others? What are those lies?

Scripture

John 10   Romans 8:1
John 14:6   2 Corinthians 4:2

> Romans 8:1 – There remains no accusing voice of condemnation against those who are joined in life-union with Jesus, the Anointed One (TPT).

10

THE TREE OF SELF-SUFFICIENCY: JUDGING GOOD AND EVIL

THE TRUTH

I KNEW THAT EATING FROM THE TREE OF THE Knowledge of Good and Evil would open Adam and Eve's eyes to that which would bring calamity to mankind until the end of the age. Thus, they would become their own god and would be the judge of good and evil (right and wrong) for themselves. Therefore, they would no longer trust Me to decide that for them. After biting the fruit of the Tree of Knowledge of Good and Evil, one of the first acts of Adam and Eve was to judge that being naked and vulnerable was evil. They judged themselves as unacceptable and covered up. You are no different when you choose to live out of the lies of your flesh (your self-sufficient ways). You believe the lie; you feel worthless, unacceptable, unlovable, and insecure, and you make that your truth by agreeing with it. Then, you do something to hide and self-protect. That lie results in unrighteous behavior. Or, you believe you are self-sufficient, not needing Me or others, and set out to live in those lies that drive your fleshly ways. That lie results in self-righteous behavior. In the coming days, I want to untwist that lie and bring it to Truth so that you will recognize it in the future. I want you to turn to Me, not the ways of the flesh. I will reveal this to you as you seek Me.

The Question

What lies are you tempted to believe about yourself on an emotional level that do not line up with who God says you are?

Scripture

Genesis 2:9, 17   Genesis 3:1-8   Isaiah 53:6

Appendix B: Who I Am in Christ

Isaiah 53:6 - ...Each of us has turned from God's paths and chosen our own way...(TPT).

11

RENEWING THE MIND: TRUTH THAT SETS YOU FREE

THE TRUTH

ADAM AND EVE WALKED WITH US (FATHER, Son, and Holy Spirit) in perfect harmony and bliss. They had everything in their union with Us. They stumbled and fell when they believed Satan's lie that they could be like God. Thus, entered their attempt, which has become your attempt, to meet God-given needs for love, acceptance, worth, and security apart from Me. Although you have given your heart to Jesus, the Evil One will tempt you to believe the lies that distort your view of God, yourself, and others. Despite the fact that your old man, with his sinful nature, was crucified on the cross, your mind is in the process of being renewed to Truth. Therefore, the lies activate your Flesh (trying to meet your God-given needs apart from Christ). Only the Truth will set you free. I will illumine the path of Life for you. Your only work is to believe Jesus—Who He says He is and who He says you are. Seek to find who Jesus says you are. I will reveal that through the

Scriptures and the Rhema word spoken directly to your mind.

THE QUESTIONS

Who do you believe Jesus is? Who do you believe you are?

SCRIPTURE

Genesis 3:5	John 6:28-29	Galatians 2:20 (TPT)
Genesis 1:26,27	Romans 12:1-2	Colossians 1:15

Appendix A: The God of the Bible
Appendix B: Who I Am in Christ

Colossians 1:15 – He is the divine portrait, the true likeness of the invisible God...

12

DISTORTED LOVE: HOW LIES BLOCK INTIMACY

THE TRUTH

I HAVE TOLD YOU TO LOVE THE LORD YOUR God with all your heart, soul, strength, and mind, and your neighbor as yourself. Your life circumstances, authority figures, and relationships have formed your view of Me, yourself, and others. As you look back over your life, you will see where you began to be tempted to believe the lies that will block you from believing and receiving My Love. That keeps you from being able to love Me, yourself, and others. The Evil One, Satan, is a liar; Diablos is his name. He wants you to base your truth on that which is contrary to what I say about Myself, you, and others—The Truth. I will unravel all this, removing the blocks and exposing the lies so you can walk freely in My Light, which is Life. Seek Me! The answers are there for you!

The Question

What are you tempted to believe about yourself that has been formed from relationships, circumstances, or rejections?

Scripture

Genesis 3:1-8   Psalm 27:8
Luke 10:27   John 8:12

Appendix B: Who I Am in Christ

Genesis 3:7 – Immediately, their eyes were opened…so they sewed fig leaves together for coverings (TPT).

13

THE GIFT OF RIGHTEOUS

THE TRUTH

BECAUSE YOU ARE MINE, I WILL SHOW YOU your righteousness. It is one of the most precious gifts given to you by Me. The gift of righteousness was given at the cross when Jesus became sin for you and took your punishment. You were crucified with Him. He raised you to new life. He is in you, and you are in Him. He is in you to be your new Life, evidenced by giving you His nature. Furthermore, He has totally replaced your old dead human spirit with its sinful nature with His nature, bearing His characteristics and attributes, especially His righteousness. Because you are no longer identified with sin, through your lens of righteousness, you can see the lies you have believed that have caused you to choose your flesh. The lies always lead you to sin, turning to your fleshly ways instead of faith and total dependence on Christ. I will untwist the lie as you begin to choose to believe who you are in Christ.

THE QUESTIONS

When did you first believe a lie about yourself contrary to who Christ says you are? What is that lie?

SCRIPTURE

Isaiah 53:6	Romans 5:17 (TPT)	Romans 6:4
Romans 7:6 (TPT)	Galatians 2:20 TPT)	Colossians 2:6-7 (TPT)

Appendix B: Who I Am in Christ

Romans 5:17 - ...how much more are we held in the grip of grace and continue reigning as kings in life...(TPT).

14

PERFORMANCE AND WORTH: BREAKING THE LIE

THE TRUTH

IF YOU WERE RAISED TO BELIEVE YOUR WORTH was only in what you did, you will continue to believe you are worthless or unacceptable unless you perform. The performance becomes a measure of your value, a way of feeling secure in situations, a way to get love plus acceptance, the unconditional love we all want and need. You, over time, unknowingly set yourself up as your own god, judging good and evil, right and wrong for yourself. Your truth is not The Truth as set down for you in Scripture, the Living Word of Jesus Christ. You seem to always believe something is missing according to your feelings. That "something" drives you to meet your needs with your own strength and resources. Your coping mechanisms, defense mechanisms, flesh, and habitual sin patterns are set at a very early age because your perception has been warped by how you see the authority figures in your life, the circumstances, and the rejections that have come your way. Your "life messages" are believable to you because they come complete with feelings. Your coping is simply a means to get out of pain or prove yourself because of what you believe. I can show you the root of your unbelief that keeps you from The Truth as you surrender your way. I will be the Light for your path. Follow me.

The Questions

Are you ready to choose and surrender to Spirit (My Way) over flesh (your way)? Are there any blocks to your surrendering to My Way? If so, what are they?

Scripture

Proverbs 3:5-6   Genesis 3:5   Galatians 5:19-21
Psalm 119:105   Isaiah 30:18-22

Appendix C: Prayer of Surrender

Proverbs 3:5 – …With all your heart rely on Him
to guide you (TPT).

15

Self-righteousness: The Hidden Bondage

THE TRUTH

IF YOU WERE RAISED TO THINK YOU ARE BETTER than others, you will live a life of self-righteousness, judging, criticizing, and living self-centeredly. This will block your vision of even seeing a need for God in your life. You have been caught in the same deceitful web as Adam and Eve. You have made yourself your god. Your adequacy is in yourself and your accomplishments. Although you have salvation, you live much like the Pharisees (under the Law). I am faithful to show you the deceit and denial that keep you disconnected from God, His will, your own heart, and the hearts of others. Come to Me! Only I can set you free with the Truth. My job is to shine The Light on the darkness caused by the lies.

THE QUESTION

What were you raised to believe about yourself?

Scripture

John 5:37-40
2 Corinthians 3:5 (TPT)
Philippians 3:5-8 (TPT)

> John 5:39-40…You are busy analyzing the Scriptures…yet you still refuse to come to Me…

16

FROM SELF-SUFFICIENCY TO LIVING WATER

THE TRUTH

DO NOT LOOK AT YOUR BEHAVIOR. YOU ARE constantly adjusting that to please others or render yourself acceptable. Look for the stronghold of lies through which your thoughts are filtered. If you believe you are better than others, your lie system will tell you that you are self-sufficient and can do anything in your own strength. That same lie system says you do not need God because you can handle your life by yourself. As far as others are concerned, you will see them as "less than." There is no relationship or intimacy in any of those lies. Do not forget that God created you for His purposes, but above all, for a relationship and intimacy that you cannot even imagine with Himself and others. Are you tired of living a self-righteous life? You are born again and have your salvation, but are the lies blocking the Fountain of Life from flowing through you? If you are thirsty, I am here to take you to the only One Who can give you Living Water, where you will never thirst again.

THE QUESTIONS

As I have revealed the lies about your self-sufficiency, are you willing to come to Me so I can reveal the Truth about who you are and your desperate need for Me? What lies might try to block you from coming to Me?

SCRIPTURE

Psalm 36:9   John 4:10-11   John 7:38
2 Corinthians 10:3-5   Ephesians 2:10

John 7:38 – Believe in Me so that rivers of living water will burst out from within you…(TPT).

17

WHO DO YOU SAY I AM: RECEIVING YOUR TRUE IDENTITY

THE TRUTH

AS YOU SEEK MY FACE (REQUIRE ME AS A VITAL necessity in your life), you will increasingly understand that I will reveal how God defines who you are. Relationships, circumstances, and rejections all try to have a voice in your life. If you agree with the messages (lies) spoken to you about Who I am or who you are or your need for others to meet your God-given needs, you will end up asking yourself the questions, "Who am I?" and "What am I going to do?" These questions always lead you back to your flesh (your comfort zone of coping apart from total dependence on Jesus Christ). If you will stop and ask Me, I will remind you of Who Jesus says you are. He died, giving His body that you might have new life, thus a new identity. I want you to receive and believe The Truth of who God says you are. It will begin the most intimate relationship. One that is far more than you could ask, think, or dare to imagine.

THE QUESTION

Is there anything that would keep you from being ready to ask Me who I say you are? What is it?

SCRIPTURE

Psalm 27:8 (AMPC)	John 6:28-29	2 Corinthians 5:17
Ezekiel 36:26	Ephesians 3:20-21	

Appendix B: Who I Am in Christ

2 Corinthians 5:17...if anyone is enfolded into Christ, he has become an entirely new person...(TPT).

18

CONVICTED OF RIGHTEOUSNESS, NOT CONDEMNED BY SIN

THE TRUTH

YOU MAY ASK, "HOW CAN I NOT FOCUS ON MY behavior when I know it is sinful?" I am here to convict you of your righteousness. Through your righteousness, I show you the behavior that does not line up with who you are, a new creation with the nature, attributes, and characteristics of Christ. If you have been raised or taught in church to be sin-focused, this new way of looking at Jesus may not feel comfortable at first. But the more you focus on Me, the Spirit, the more I will show you that any other way of thinking brings bondage. Focusing on sin, which Jesus became for you on the cross, will always lead you to try to do something about it. It raises the fleshly question, "What will I do?" I will lead you to totally depend on Christ by asking," God, what do You want to do, and what do You want to do through me?" And you declaring, "I am your willing servant—ready to surrender and obey."

The Questions

Is there anything keeping you from being willing to ask Jesus to live through you, moment by moment, and surrender to what He wants? If so, what is it?

Scripture

John 16:13-15 (TPT)   Proverbs 3:5-6   Romans 3:21-26 (TPT)
Romans 8:2, 5   2 Corinthians 5:21   Philippians 3:9
(TPT)

Appendix C: Prayer of Surrender

2 Corinthians 5:21 – For God made the only one who did not know sin to become sin for us, so that we might become the righteousness of God…

19

AGREEING WITH GOD
AFTER FAILURE

THE TRUTH

YOU MAY ASK, "THEN, WHAT DO I DO WITH MY sin?" Your first step is to take words to and agree with Me about your union, your loving relationship, with Me. I want you to acknowledge that you are not acting like who you are, a righteous saint. I will always love you and speak the Truth to you in order for you to know what you are believing (the fleshly lie that led you to unbelief, therefore, to sin). As you exchange that lie, I reveal the Truth that I want you to walk in. You are already forgiven, so you can agree with the Truth I reveal. You can come into agreement with Me that you believed a lie that affected your behavior. Right believing equals right behavior. There is no condemnation for your sin. There is no punishment, only the loving response of the Heavenly Father. I want you to receive your righteousness, right standing with God, and respond out of who you are, your true identity. Righteousness is the one-time gift for all times to you. We love you!

THE QUESTION

Do you believe you are a righteous saint as you approach the throne of God, or do you believe that you are an unrighteous sinner? Please explain your answer.

SCRIPTURE

Hosea 14:1-2	Romans 3:26	Romans 4:5 (TPT)
Romans 8:1	1 Corinthians 1:30	Ephesians 1:7-8 (TPT)

Appendix B: Who I Am in Christ

Ephesians 1:7 – Since we are now joined to Christ…(we have) total cancellation of our sins…

20

LIVING FREE: FORGIVEN AND COMPLETE IN CHRIST

THE TRUTH

MY RESPONSIBILITY IS TO SHOW YOU YOUR Gift of righteousness and reveal to you what God intended for you in giving you that gift. I want you to arise every morning, free of worries, anxieties, and guilt, because you understand who you are in Christ—a righteous saint. Also, you have received the truth that you are forgiven once and for all time. The work has been done by Christ on the cross (forgiveness and a new identity). You can do **nothing** to make yourself more righteous, holy, and forgiven. **Your behavior no longer defines you; the finished work of the cross does.** If the Truth of the cross is authentic to you in your everyday walk and you depend on that Truth, you will understand just how free you are as you daily learn to depend on Christ to make every move and decision. He will speak through you and be the only One Who completely fulfills you. All Jesus asks is that you believe!

THE QUESTIONS

What is blocking you from receiving/believing these Truths? What is the lie that often plagues you and keeps you from believing in your union with Christ?

SCRIPTURE

John 6:28-29   Acts 17:28   Isaiah 60:1 (AMPC)
2 Corinthians 5:21   Mark 4:24-25 (TPT)

Appendix B: Who I Am in Christ

Mark 4:25 – For those who listen with open hearts will receive more revelation… (TPT).

21

THE WAR WITHIN: FLESH, WORLD, AND THE ENEMY

THE TRUTH

AS YOU ASK, "WHAT COULD BLOCK ME FROM the Truth?" Truth is Jesus- "the Way, the Truth, and the Life." Many things will try to keep you from Jesus. The Word says that the world, the flesh, and the devil will constantly war with your walk in the Spirit. The world wants you to look through the lens of "the lust of the flesh, the lust of the eyes, and the pride of life." Trust Me to reveal the lies that keep you choosing your flesh, which cause you to crave only sensual gratification; the person or things that you go after to fulfill a place in you that only Jesus can; and the "way" you think might be better than the plan God has for you to make you and mold you into the image of Christ Jesus. Your way only leads you to your own resources and strength, trying to live a life apart from Christ that you were never meant to lead.

The Question

What is the recurring lie that tempts you not to walk in the Spirit?

Scripture

Jeremiah 29:11-13   John 14:6   Galatians 5:16-18
Ephesians 6:12   2 John 2:15-16   1 John 5:18-20 (TPT)
Proverbs 3:5-6

> Proverbs 3:5 – Lean on, trust in, and be confident
> in the Lord…do not rely on your own insight or
> understanding…

22

A DISTORTED VIEW OF GOD

THE TRUTH

THE FALL OF MAN RESULTED IN ADAM CHOOSING Eve over God to meet His need for love, acceptance, worth, and security. When Eve was deceived by Satan, believing that she could "be like God, knowing the difference between good and evil and blessing and calamity," she was somehow changed in that moment. Therefore, Adam chose her over God as his all-in-all and his enough. He abandoned the relationship he had with God—intimate, personal, and vulnerable. God had been Adam's "All in All and his Enough." He had such a personal relationship with God that he was given responsibility over all creation and walked and talked with God. God created Eve, especially for Adam, to be his "Isha" (Adam's woman). Now, because of Adam's choice, all of humanity would pay the price of being born into sin, a sinner by nature. From this, even after salvation and the realization that we have the nature of Christ and no longer a sinful nature, everyone is

tempted to believe a lie about God according to their former Adamic nature, their programming by an authority figure (usually Dad), and circumstances.

THE QUESTION

What distorted view of God are you tempted to believe so that the lie can be brought to Truth?

SCRIPTURE

Genesis 3:5   1 Corinthians 15:28   Ephesians 4:5-6 (TPT)

Appendix A: The God of the Bible

Genesis 3:8 – Then Adam and his wife heard the sound of YAHWEH-God passing through the garden…so, they hid among the trees…(TPT).

23

"Where Are You?": God's Invitation to Relationship

THE TRUTH

IN GENESIS 3, IT IS REVEALED THAT SATAN'S mission to deceive humanity is in place. Adam and Eve believed his lies and "bit the apple." With their choice, a lie about Who God is was believed according to how they thought He would react to their sin. It is evident that as God walks through the Garden to find them, He asks one of the most intimate questions in all of Scripture, "Where are you?" Of course, He knew where they were, but we see the deceit at work as they hide from God. Their judgment of God is in place. As sin and fear clouded their vision, they believed He must be an angry, punishing, judgmental God and One who must be hidden from when one sins. It is essential for you to let Me reveal to you your distorted view of God that encourages you to believe a lie about Him. Now, when you sin, you will not hide from God but run to Him, believing He is Who He says He is—a forgiving, loving Father.

The Questions

Are you ready to exchange your distorted view of God and receive the Truth that will set you free to believe Scriptural Truth about God? What is the Truth that God is revealing to you?

Scripture

Genesis 3:8-9   Hebrews 4:16 (TPT)   Isaiah 44:6 (TPT)
John 14:6   Hosea 14:2

> Hebrews 4:16 – So now we draw near freely and boldly to where grace is enthroned…(TPT).

24

UNION WITH CHRIST: HIS LIFE LIVED THROUGH YOU

THE TRUTH

ON THE CROSS, JESUS NOT ONLY GAVE HIS blood to wash you clean of all sin for all time, but He gave His body so I, the Holy Spirit, could come into union with you and live My life through you as you. I brought your dead human spirit back to life, and My power completes and seals Your union. This means you are one with Me and bear My identification. This union not only gives you My Nature but also My characteristics and attributes. Because of that timeless truth, for you to live in this world, you are whatever I am, except deity. To walk in truly who and Whose you are in this world, the distortions you are tempted to believe must be brought to Truth. That necessary part of your healing keeps the enemy from trying to steal, kill, and destroy you on any front as you walk by faith, not by sight.

The Question

What is blocking you from being ready to receive and believe the scriptural Truth about Who I am and who you are so that you can live totally dependent on Me?

Scripture

Ephesians 1:13	1 John 4:17c	Galatians 2:20 (TPT)
Romans 6:3-14	John 10:10	2 Corinthians 5:7 (TPT)

Appendix A: The God of the Bible

Galatians 2:20 – ...And now the essence of this new life is no longer mine for the Anointed One lives His life through me—we live in union as one! (TPT).

25

Everything for Life and Godliness

THE TRUTH

JESUS EXCHANGED HIS LIFE FOR YOURS ON THE cross by giving you His Spirit (nature, characteristics, and attributes) for your dead human spirit. Understanding the power this Truth gives you to walk in this world is necessary for daily victory over the lies that encourage you to rely on self-sufficiency. Satan twisted and distorted the Truth of Who I am, and He also twisted your concept of who you are. Jesus asks one thing of you. Believe! Believe Who He says He is, and believe who He says you are. It is time to stand by faith in the Truth of who Jesus says you are and not according to what you have done, how someone else has identified you, or your feelings. As a New Covenant believer, you have been given everything for life and godliness to live on this earth. Jesus has made it possible for you to share in His divine nature because of the finished work of the cross. The Truth will set you free from the past, allow you to focus on the present moment, and live free of all distortions.

THE QUESTIONS

Are you ready to live in My power and experience the ultimate healing, which is exchanging distorted lies and feelings for scriptural Truth? What might that healing look like?

SCRIPTURE

John 6:28-29   2 Peter 1:3-4   Ephesians 6:14
Ephesians 2:10, TPT

Appendix B: Who I Am in Christ

2 Peter 1:3 – Everything we could ever need for life and godliness has already been deposited in us by His divine power…

26

Hearing God's Voice Moment by Moment

THE TRUTH

NOW THAT YOU DESIRE TO LIVE IN THE truth of Who God is and who you are, it is essential to recognize the voice of God and believe what He says as you seek Him on a moment-by-moment basis. God has provided a plethora of ways in which He speaks to you: Scripture, Rhema (spoken by His Spirit), nature, others, praise, and worship, to name a few. There are four questions to ask God that will keep you on the track of Truth:

1. God, Who do I need you to be in this moment? (Comforter, Provider, Healer, etc.)

2. God, how do You want to love me today?

3. God, how do You want to love others through me today?

4. God, what do You want to do, and how
   much of it do You want to do through me?

THE QUESTIONS

Are you willing to walk the track of Truth in order to experience Christ as your life? Is there anything blocking you from asking God these four questions? If so, what might those blocks be?

SCRIPTURE

John 10:4, 14   Psalm 27:8   Matthew 22:36-39
John 15:5

John 10:4 - ...He walks ahead of them (sheep) and they will follow him, for they are familiar with his voice...(TPT).

27

THE FREEDOM OF SURRENDER

THE TRUTH

SURRENDERING OR YIELDING TO GOD MEANS being free to give over to Him what you're holding onto that would cause you not to walk in His Way. That act embraces God's perspective in your relationships, circumstances, and worldly goods, as they all belong to Him and are under His care. You are simply a steward of all that you have from Him. Taking God's lead in what He wants to do in and through you will offer you a life of grace, mercy, love, and freedom. Letting Me reveal what you need to release to Me continually is a necessary step in your journey to knowing and experiencing Me as your Enough.

THE QUESTION

What do you need to surrender to Me so you can walk in freedom and deeper intimacy with Me and others?

SCRIPTURE

Psalm 46:10   Isaiah 30:18-22   Job 11:13-19 (NIV)
Romans 12:1 (MSG)   Luke 5:5-11   Isaiah 50:10-11

Appendix C: Prayer of Surrender

Psalm 46:10 – Surrender your anxiety. Be still and realize that I am God…(TPT).

28

FORGIVENESS: RELEASING THE BLOCK TO FREEDOM

THE TRUTH

SURRENDERING TO GOD IS TO COME INTO agreement with your union with Christ. It is believing and receiving the truths of the New Covenant so you can live free of the lust of the flesh, the lust of the eyes, and the pride of life. As you walk in the freedom of who you are, God will call you to live from your obedient heart. Unforgiveness is a significant block to living free (dead to sin and alive to Christ). To experience epignosis, the complete and perfect knowledge of God, taking part in the finished work of the cross is essential. You must unite yourself with the cleansing, powerful blood of Jesus in forgiving those who have sinned against you and releasing God and yourself from anything you are holding onto. God will make known to you what He wants to give you in exchange for what you have stored in your mind against God, yourself, and others.

THE QUESTION

What blocks are holding you back from freely forgiving so you can live from Truth rather than your feelings?

SCRIPTURE

1 John 2:15-17   Romans 6:17 (TPT)   Romans 8:9-10
Colossians 3:13   Ephesians 4:31-32 (TPT)
Matthew 18:21-22   Ephesians 1:7

Appendix C: Prayer of Surrender
Appendix E: Forgiveness

Colossians 3:13 - ...forgive(ing) one another in the same way you have been graciously forgiven by Jesus Christ...(TPT).

29

The Exchange That Heals Relationships

THE TRUTH

THERE ARE FOUR ESSENTIAL ELEMENTS TO forgiveness. Allowing God to reveal the offenses you are holding onto and the feelings that accompany them is vital to walking in freedom. Exchanging the lie you have believed about yourself, God, or others is another step. The ultimate desire of God is to give you an exchange for all you are giving Him. To walk in forgiveness, God has given you the power to choose by an act of your will to believe in the Truth of who you are in Christ. Regardless of the severity of the offense or how you feel about it, He is asking you to choose the truth—**you are a forgiver by nature**. Allowing God to reveal all four parts to you will release you from the bondage you have walked in.

4 steps to forgiveness:

1. Release the offenses and feelings to God.

2. Exchange your offenses and feelings for what God wants you to have.

3. Break the judgments you have placed on
   God, another or yourself.

4. Exchange the lie you have believed about
   God, self, or others for Truth.

The Questions

Do you want to be free to walk in Truth? What keeps you from being willing to get in touch with the pain of broken relationships in order to experience who you are—a forgiver?

Scripture

Matthew 18:22 Colossians 2:12-14 (TPT)
Ephesians 4:32 Colossians 3:12-13
Ephesians 4:26

Appendix E: Forgiveness

Colossians 2:13 - ...for we are forever alive and forgiven of all our sins (TPT)!

30

FORGIVENESS AS A WAY OF LIFE

THE TRUTH

CHOOSING TO SURRENDER AND FORGIVE defeats the enemy. He is trying to steal, kill, and destroy all believers. The choice to live in freedom by receiving and believing the exchanges God has for you will empower you to choose to relate in a healthy and loving way with God, yourself, and others. These necessary components of forgiveness are not a one-time exercise. Whenever offenses occur, you must quickly come to the Father and walk through the elements of forgiveness. Every hurtful occurrence is your invitation to intimacy with Him. The Father longs to embrace you and take the lies and pain from you caused by the offenses. He will always give you fresh, new exchanges to nurture your heart.

THE QUESTION

What might be keeping you from living out of feelings and choosing by your will and the power of the Spirit to walk in forgiveness?

SCRIPTURE

John 10:10	Matthew 22:37-40	Psalm 13
Isaiah 61:3	Matthew 18:21-22	

Appendix E: Forgiveness

Psalm 13:2,5 – (How long must I) have sorrow in my heart day after day…But I have trusted, leaned on, and been confident in your mercy and lovingkindness…

31

Forgiveness and the Whole Person: Spirit, Soul, and Body

THE TRUTH

THE BEAUTY OF FORGIVENESS IS ITS POWERFUL benefits. Because you are a three-part being (spirit, soul, and body), you must consider how forgiveness affects each part. To forgive is to live from the Spirit in walking in who and Whose you are. You are a forgiver because of your new nature, Christ's nature living in and through you, as you. The soul (mind, will, and emotions) chooses Spirit or flesh. In choosing Life and The Way, not flesh and your way, the forgiveness muscle is strengthened. Your body will benefit from letting go of the past with its hurts. You can heal and walk forward in truth without the self-righteous pride, anger, resentment, and hurt controlling you. You are a forgiver. As you forgive, your body releases the negativity that is so very unhealthy. What freedom awaits you!

THE QUESTION

What keeps you from being willing to exercise Truth by choosing as an act of your soul what God has already done in your spirit?

SCRIPTURE

1 Thessalonians 5:23   Galatians 5:16   Romans 6:4-6 (TPT)
Romans 6:11

Appendix E: Forgiveness

1 Thessalonians 5:23 - …may your spirit and soul and body be preserved sound and complete…at the coming of our Lord Jesus Christ…

32

ENTERING GOD'S REST: IT IS FINISHED

THE TRUTH

GOD ASSURES YOU THAT YOUR FAITH ACTIVATES the promise of confident rest. You can enter into rest because Jesus completed all work on your behalf and declared, "It is finished!" What is finished? You are! Jesus has given you everything for life and godliness for eternity because you are in union, one, with Him. He has fulfilled all that was written about Himself. He has also promised to remove all obstacles to your understanding of the sanctification process because it is His work to make and mold you into the image of Jesus Christ. Your security is in Christ Jesus alone. No matter what, you are loved, righteous, holy, forgiven, and blameless because of the finished work of the cross. Resting comes from believing and receiving the truth by not creating anything you think needs to be added to this work. It is truly finished!

More Than Forgiven The Question

What stands in the way and causes you to believe you lack something from God that keeps you from believing, therefore, resting in the finished work of the cross?

Scripture

Hebrews 4:1	John 19:30	2 Peter 1:3-4	Matthew 5:17-18
Ephesians 3:20	I Thessalonians 5:24	2 Corinthians 3:18 (TPT)	

Appendix F: Completed Works of Christ

1 Thessalonians 5:24 - …(He) will thoroughly complete His work in you (TPT).

33

COMPLETE IN CHRIST: NOTHING MISSING, NOTHING BROKEN

THE TRUTH

BELIEVING IN THE REVELATION OF WHO YOU are in Christ and Who He is in you is the first step to resting in the finished work of the cross. Knowing you are whole, complete with every good and perfect gift from the Heavenly Father, brings the reality of having all your needs for love, acceptance, worth, and security fulfilled in Christ alone. This is a finished work. This is nothing anyone could have ever accomplished for you, or you could have done in your own strength. Jesus gave His life as a ransom for your life for eternity. He did this so you could live free with no bondage to your past, relationships, or circumstances. He exchanged His life, complete with His characteristics and attributes, for your life so He could live through you, as you (union). He began that good work of sanctification in you, and He promises to complete it. He simply asks you to believe and receive the fact that He wants to live each moment of your earthly life in and through you. That will bring you to a place of resting in Christ because of the finished work of the cross.

The Question

What thoughts might you believe that place doubt in the finished work of the cross and all Christ has done for you?

Scripture

Colossians 2:10	James 1:17 (TPT)	1 John 4:17
Ephesians 1:5-6	Psalm 139:13-14	Ephesians 2:20-22
Ephesians 5:1 (TPT)	Galatians 2:20	Romans 6:3-6
Philippians 1:6	John 6:28-29	

Appendix A: The God of the Bible
Appendix B: Who I Am in Christ

1 John 4:17c - ...all that Jesus now is, so are we in this world (TPT).

34

ESTABLISHED IN TRUTH: STANDING IN FAITH

THE TRUTH

WITH EVERY TRUTH GOD REVEALS TO YOU, there will be a time of establishment. There may be a problematic situation, relationship, or circumstance in life where God asks you to trust (a measure of belief) Him and His Way. The opposite of this is turning to familiar flesh patterns, worldly thinking, or an agreement with the enemy (your way). God is asking you to stand believing by faith in the finished work of the cross and all He has done to set you free so that you can rest in Him. Resting in Christ is difficult because your feelings will fight for the right to be valid unless you base your thoughts on Scriptural Truth. Feelings always follow what you are thinking. Therefore, with your thoughts based on Truth, it is an excellent time to surrender what you are holding onto in order to grasp what God has for you in the true rest of your soul.

THE QUESTIONS

What is blocking you from believing in your union with Christ? Are you ready to receive, by faith, every opportunity to live from this union? What might that look like?

SCRIPTURE

John 6:28-29   I Peter 5:10   2 Corinthians 5:7
John 5:6 (TPT with footnote)   1 John 2:15-17

Appendix G: Union with Christ

1 Peter 5:10 - …the God…Who has called you to His own…will Himself complete and make you what you ought to be, establish you…

35

THE EXCHANGED LIFE: CHRIST LIVING THROUGH YOU

THE TRUTH

AS A NEW COVENANT BELIEVER, YOU LIVE AN exchanged life with Jesus by faith. He accomplished that for you on the cross in your co-crucifixion with Him. Your "old man," with its sinful nature, has been exchanged for Christ's nature. That nature exchange came complete with His attributes and characteristics. Therefore, you became a new creation. That exchange also came with everything for life and godliness and your God-given needs (love, acceptance, worth, and security) fulfilled in Christ. The only work required of you is to believe that nothing is to be done except what Christ wants to do in and through you in this world. He desires you to live from His Life. He has given you an obedient heart and everything you need to come into agreement with what He wants to do through you. He will establish you in those Truths by the power of the Holy Spirit.

THE QUESTION

What might be standing in the way of your willingness to give up your way of doing things apart from total dependence on Jesus so you can live in true soul rest?

SCRIPTURE

Galatians 2:20 (TPT)   2 Peter 1:3-4   2 Peter 1:12
Hebrews 3:19   Hosea 14:2

Appendix F: Completed Works of Christ

Hebrews 3:19 – It is clear that they could not enter into their inheritance because they wrapped their hearts in unbelief (TPT).

36

THE SOVEREIGNTY OF GOD: TRUSTING HIS PLAN

THE TRUTH

BELIEF IN JESUS CHRIST AS THE WAY LEADS you to the revelation of God's sovereignty. El Elyon, The Most High God, designates Himself as the sovereign ruler of the universe. If you are to experience Him as the One True God, you must bow to Him, and all He is offering you as He makes you and molds you into the image of Jesus Christ. That is His purpose and plan for your life. As you receive that and put aside your way of thinking and doing, you will see the magnificence of His glorious sovereignty. He created you complete with a plan established before the foundation of the world. You have a choice to believe and walk this life by the Spirit or continue to believe distorted lies about God, self, and others and walk this life in the flesh, your own way.

The Question

What are the lies blocking you from believing that God, in His Sovereignty, has a plan to complete the work He began in you?

Scripture

John 14:6

Isaiah 46:9-11

Daniel 2:20-23

Deuteronomy 32:39

Isaiah 45:6-7

Isaiah 55:8-9

2 Corinthians 3:18 (TPT)

Galatians 5:16-26

Isaiah 30:18-22

Ephesians 3:20-21

Appendix A: The God of the Bible

2 Corinthians 3:18 – All of us…are constantly being transfigured into His very own image…

37

THE HEALING POWER OF GOD'S PROMISES

THE TRUTH

TO BELIEVE IN GOD'S SOVEREIGNTY OPENS THE door for you to trust His character and attributes. His sovereignty comes complete with many promises. Believing those promises by faith will enable you to set your mind on the Truth—God's Way, Jesus Christ. His plan is to remove all blocks from you: flesh, worldly thinking, and your agreement with the enemy's lies. As God reveals and establishes you in these Truths, you will realize that Truth brings the healing you long for. This healing is encompassed in His unconditional love, grace, and mercy. All you are truly looking for is the unconditional love of Christ. I, the Holy Spirit, will guide you to that Truth as no other attempt will succeed.

THE QUESTIONS

Can you see that your attempts to meet your God-given needs in your own way have failed to lead you to the purity of unconditional love, acceptance, worth, and security that only Christ offers you? How have you attempted to meet those needs in your own strength?

SCRIPTURE

Philippians 1:6   John 6:28-29   John 8:32
Psalms 138:8   1 John 5:14

Appendix A: The God of the Bible

Philippians 1:6 - ...He Who began a good work in you will continue until the day of Jesus Christ...

38

ESTABLISHED THROUGH TRIALS: JESUS IS ENOUGH

THE TRUTH

THE REVELATION OF TRUTH (A PERSON, JESUS Christ) by Me, the Holy Spirit, is solidified in your soul (mind, will, and emotions) by what God allows in your life to establish you in the Truth that Jesus is Enough. All revelation and establishment lead to the Sovereignty of God. You live in a fallen world where Satan has been given a certain amount of power. Greater is God, the Son, and the Holy Spirit in you than any power or authority Satan tries to convince you he has over you. As you stand in that Truth and seek God step by step in your life, moment by moment, you will realize His power and authority stand for all time as He reveals His perfect plan for your life. You benefit from My fruit as you walk in the Truth.

THE QUESTION

In what areas of your life are you tempted to agree with the enemy instead of God's Truth and sovereignty?

SCRIPTURE

John 14:6	Ephesians 1:4	1 Peter 1:18-20
1 Peter 1:6-9	1 John 4:4	Galatians 5:22-23
John 3:15	1 Peter 3:9	

Appendix A: The God of the Bible

John 14:6 – I am the…Truth…

39

TRUSTING THE FINISHED WORK

THE TRUTH

TRUST IS THE EXERCISE OF WORKING OUT your belief by faith. Hear this good news! The only work Jesus left for you to do is to believe Him whom the Father sent. He is the exact representation of the Father. You are to believe in your union, Christ in you and you in Christ. There is no stone unturned in the completed work of Christ. That is why you can do nothing to take away or add to what Christ has done on the cross. Christ exclaimed, "It is finished!" with His dying breath. Nothing is left for you to do except what Jesus wants to do in and through you on this earth. Even at that, whatever He asks you to do, it will be with His words, power, strength, and, above all, His love pouring forth from your union with Him as you totally depend on Him. Trust is your agreement with Jesus that His work is enough to complete you.

THE QUESTION

What might be standing in your way of agreeing with Jesus that He is your Enough in every situation?

SCRIPTURE

| John 6:28-29 | Colossians 1 | Romans 6:3-8 |
| John 19:28-30 | Hebrews 3:19 | |

Appendix G: Union with Christ

> Colossians 1:10 – We pray that you would walk in the ways of true righteousness…you'll become fruit-bearing branches, yielding to His life, and maturing in the rich experience of knowing God in His fullness (TPT).

40

LIVING THE ABUNDANT LIFE: RESTING IN CHRIST FOREVER

THE TRUTH

BECAUSE YOU ARE COMPLETE IN ME, I HAVE presented you to the Father without spot or wrinkle; without any blemishes or sin. You are seated in the heavenlies at the right hand of the Father. He sees you complete in Christ. That is your position. Your condition on this earth is governed by My making known to you through your soul (mind, will, and emotions) what Jesus has already done in your spirit, which has sealed you as one with His Spirit. God desires for you to believe Jesus, trust the finished work of the cross, and rest for all eternity, no matter what this fallen world brings to you. You can live with your mind set on things above, where you will see from the vantage point of the Spirit realm. With that view, you will know you are perfectly loved, accepted, worthy, and secure now and for all eternity! That is the Abundant Life of Victorious Living in Christ!

THE QUESTION

By faith, are you ready to receive Christ as your Life and totally depend on Him moment by moment? State any distortions that might keep you from choosing Life in Christ.

SCRIPTURE

Colossians 2:10	Ephesians 5:26-27	Ephesians 2:6
2 Corinthians 1:22	Ephesians 1:13; 4:30	John 6:28-29
Colossians 3:2		

> Colossians 3:2 - ...feast on all the treasures of the heavenly realm...and not with the distractions of the natural realm (TPT).

Epilogue

WELL DONE! THAT WAS A LOT OF WORK IN a very short time. The Foreword suggested you would have a new understanding of your journey with Christ as you worked through **MORE THAN FORGIVEN**. I pray that it is so for you. To understand your union with Christ, Who He says He is, and who He says you are, is paramount in understanding your new life in Christ in the sanctification process. It is freedom to comprehend the finished work of the cross, and the truth that there is nothing you can do to add to or take away from that work. God wants you to enjoy the sanctification journey in this life by depending on Him in such a way that you exclaim as Paul did in Ephesians 3:20-21:

Now to Him Who, by (in consequence of) the [action of His] power that is at work within us, is able to [carry out His purpose and] do superabundantly, far over and above all that we [dare] ask or think [infinitely beyond our highest prayers, desires, thoughts, hopes, or dreams]—To Him be glory in the church and in Christ Jesus throughout all generations forever and ever. Amen (so be it) (AMPC).

What's next? Continued encouragement comes in many ways: seeking an Exchanged Life counselor to help you through difficult times by guiding you with Scriptural truth; reading Exchanged Life books; listening to podcasts and sermons from New Covenant teachers and pastors;

gathering with like-minded believers regularly are just a few suggestions to encourage your walk in union with Jesus.

There are two verses I will end with. On days when you know you need Jesus to carry you, turn to Isaiah 43:2, When you pass through the waters, I will be with you, and through the rivers, they will not overwhelm you. When you walk through the fire, you will not be burned or scorched, nor will the flame kindle upon you.

When you want God's exchange for what you are struggling with, receive Isaiah 40:31, But those who wait for the Lord [who expect, look for, and hope in Him] shall change (exchange) and renew their strength and power; they shall lift their wings and mount up [close to God] as eagles [mount up to the sun]; they shall run and not be weary, they shall walk and not faint or become tired.

Jesus wants you to benefit from the finished work of the cross by receiving all that He created you to be and all that He is as He lives in union with you as you. It is truly finished! What is the only thing "required" of you? BELIEVE!

APPENDICES

These appendices are for further study and reflection:

- Appendix A: The God of the Bible
- Appendix B: Who I Am in Christ
- Appendix C: Prayer of Surrender
- Appendix D: Assurance of a Saving Relationship with Christ
- Appendix E: Forgiveness Assignment
- Appendix F: Completed Works of Christ
- Appendix G: Our Union with Christ

Appendix A

The God of the Bible

Jeremiah 32:17 – Nothing is too difficult for Him.

Ephesians 3:20 – He is able to do immeasurably more than all we ask or imagine according to His power that is at work within us.

Romans 8:31 – If God is for us, who can be against us?

Romans 8:38–39 – Nothing in all of creation can separate us from God's love.

John 17:23 – He loves us as much as He loves Jesus.

Isaiah 40:12-31 – He will never leave us, nor forsake us.

Psalm 86:15 – He is gracious and compassionate, slow to anger and abounding in love and faithfulness.

Matthew 11:29 – He is gentle, tender, and humble in heart. He gives us rest for our souls.

Eph. 3:16-19 – His love is beyond our natural mind's ability to grasp.

John 10:14-15 – He restores our soul.

Romans 8:28 – He has everything designed to work for our good. (See Genesis 50:20.)

Romans 10:11 – No one who puts their hope in Him will be put to shame or disappointed. (See Psalm 25:3 & Isaiah 49:23c.)

Psalm 86:5 – He is kind and forgiving and abounding in love to all who call upon His name.

1 John 3:1 – He has made us His own children.

Colossians 1:13 – He has transferred us out of the kingdom of darkness and into the kingdom of His beloved Son.

1 Corinthians 1:25 – His foolishness is wiser than man's wisdom.

Psalm 91 – He is our shelter, our refuge, and our fortress.

Philippians 1:6 – He will complete the work He has begun in us.

A Look at God's Sovereignty and His Love

El Elyon – The Most High God. This name designates God as the sovereign ruler of all the universe.

Daniel 4:34-35 - For His dominion is an everlasting dominion, and His kingdom endures from generation to generation. And all the inhabitants of the earth are accounted as nothing, but He does according to His will in the host of heaven and among the inhabitants of earth; and no one can ward off His hand or say to Him, "What hast Thou done?"

Isaiah 14:24-27 - The Lord of hosts has sworn saying, "Surely just as I have intended so it has happened, and just as I have planned so it will stand, to break Assyria in My land, and I will trample him on My mountains. Then his yoke will be removed from them, and his burden removed from their shoulder. This is the plan devised against the whole earth; and this is the hand that is stretched out against all the nations. For the Lord of hosts has planned, and who can frustrate it? And as for His stretched-out hand, who can turn it back?"

Isaiah 46:9-11 - "For I am God, and there is no other; I am God, and there is no one like me, Declaring the end from the beginning and from ancient times things which have not been done. Saying, 'My purpose will be established, and I will accomplish all My good pleasure; calling a bird of prey from the east, the man of My purpose from a far country. Truly I have spoken; truly I will bring it to pass. I have planned it, surely I will do it.'"

Daniel 2:20-23 - Let the name of God be blessed forever and ever, for wisdom and power belong to Him. And it is He who changes the times and the epochs; He removes kings and establishes kings; He gives wisdom to wise men and knowledge to men of understanding. It is He who reveals the profound and hidden things; He knows what is in the darkness, and the light dwells with Him. To Thee, O God of my fathers, I give thanks and praise, for Thou hast given me wisdom and power; even now Thou hast made known to me what we requested of Thee, for Thou hast made known to us the king's matter.

Deuteronomy 32:39 - "See now that I, I am He, and there is no god besides Me; it is I who put to death and give life. I have wounded, and it is I who heal; and there is no one who can deliver from My hand."

1 Samuel 1:5-6 - But to Hannah he would give a double portion, for he loved Hannah, but the Lord had closed her womb. Her rival, however, would provoke her bitterly to irritate her, because the Lord had closed her womb.

1 Samuel 2:6-10 - The Lord kills and makes alive; He brings down to Sheol and raises up. The Lord makes poor and rich; He brings low, He also exalts. He raises the poor from the dust. He lifts the needy from the ash heap to make them sit with nobles, and inherit a seat of honor; for the pillars of the earth are the Lord's, and He set the work on them. He keeps the feet of His godly ones, but the wicked ones are silenced in darkness; for not by might shall a man prevail. Those who contend with the Lord will be shattered; against them He will thunder in the heavens, the Lord will judge the ends of the earth; and He will give strength to His king, and will exalt the horn of His anointed.

Isaiah 45:6-7 - "I am the Lord, and there is no other, the One forming light and creating darkness, causing well-being and creating calamity; I am the Lord who does all these."

Job 1:8 - And the Lord said to Satan, "Have you considered my servant Job?"

Job 42:2 - "I know that Thou canst do all things, And that no purpose of Thine can be thwarted."

Luke 22:31 - "Simon, Simon, behold, Satan has demanded (or obtained by asking) permission to sift you like wheat, but I have prayed for you, that your faith may not fail; and you, when once you have turned again, strengthen your brothers."

Psalms 57:2 - I will cry to God Most High, to God who accomplishes all things for me.

John 4:8,10,16,19 - ... God is love. And this is love, not that we loved God, but that He loved us and sent His Son. And we have come to know and have believed the love which God has for us. God is love, and the one who abides in love, abides in God, and God abides in him. . . We love because He first loved us.

1 Corinthians 13:4-8 - Love is (therefore, God, Who is Love, is) patient, kind, not jealous; does not brag and is not arrogant; does not act unbecomingly; does not seek His own; is not provoked, does not take into account a wrong suffered, does not rejoice in unrighteousness but rejoices with truth; bears all things, believes all things, hopes all things, endures all things; never fails.

John 15:9 - "Just as the Father has loved Me, I have also loved you; abide in My love."

APPENDIX B

WHO I AM IN CHRIST

I am accepted in Christ

I am a child of God (John 1:12).

I am Jesus' friend (John 15:15).

I am no longer a slave, but a son/daughter (Galatians 4:5-7).

I have been adopted as a son/daughter (Romans 8:15; Ephesians 1:5).

I am a son/daughter of God and He is my Father (Romans 8:14-15; Galatians 3:26; 4:6).

I am an heir of God – a joint heir with Christ, sharing His inheritance with Him (Galatians 4:6-7; Romans 8:17).

I am united with the Lord and am one in spirit with Him (1 Corinthians 6:17).

I am saved by grace through faith and not of my works – I have nothing to boast about before God (Ephesians 2:8-9).

I have peace with God, and am reconciled to Him (2 Corinthians 5:18-19).

I am loved by Jesus and freed from my sins by His blood (Revelation 1:5).

I have been forgiven of all my sin (Colossians 2:13).

I have been washed, sanctified, and justified in the name of Jesus by the Holy Spirit (1 Corinthians 6:11).

I am a slave of God and a slave to righteousness (Romans 6:18-19, 22).

I am a fellow citizen with the rest of God's family (Ephesians 2:19).

I am a partaker of Christ; I share in His life (Hebrews 3:14).

I am one of God's living stones, being built up in Christ as a spiritual house (1 Peter 2:5).

I have been bought with a price and I belong to God (1 Corinthians 6:20).

I am dead to sin and alive to God (Romans 6:11).

I am a new creation – the old is gone, the new has come (2 Corinthians 5:17).

I am a saint (1 Corinthians 1:2; Ephesians 1:1; Philippians 1:1; Colossians 1:2).

I am righteous and holy (Ephesians 4:24).

I have been justified (Romans 5:1).

I have direct access to God through the Holy Spirit (Ephesians 2:18).

I have been redeemed and forgiven of all my sins (Colossians 1:14).

I am complete in Christ and have all I need (Colossians 2:10).

I am secure in Christ

I am free forever from condemnation (Romans 8:1-2).

I am never left alone or forsaken (Hebrews 13:5).

I am hidden with Christ in God (Colossians 3:3).

I have been established, anointed, and sealed by God (2 Corinthians 1:21-22).

I have been delivered from the domain of darkness and transferred into the Kingdom of Jesus (Colossians 1:13).

God's divine power has given me everything I need for a godly life (2 Peter 1:3).

I can resist the devil and he will flee from me (James 4:7).

God has given me spiritual weapons and spiritual armor that are mighty through God to destroy enemy strongholds (Ephesians 6:12-18; 2 Corinthians 10:4-5).

I am strong in the Lord and in the strength of His might (Ephesians 6:10).

I can stand firm against every scheme of the devil (Ephesians 6:11).

I am confident that the work God started in me, He will see through to completion (Philippians 1:6).

I have victory through Christ (1 Corinthians 15:57).

I am more than a conqueror – overwhelming victory is mine in Jesus (Romans 8:37).

I have overcome the world (1 John 5:4).

I overcome the enemy by the blood of the Lamb and the word of my testimony (Revelation 12:11).

Greater is He who is in me than He who is in the world (1 John 4:4).

I have not been given a spirit of fear, but of power, love and self-discipline (2 Timothy 1:7).

I am born of God and the evil one cannot touch me (1 John 5:18).

My name is written in heaven & I have authority to trample over every power of the enemy so that nothing shall hurt me (Luke 10:19-20).

I can find grace and mercy in my time of need, coming before God with confidence (Hebrews 4:16).

I am assured that all things work together for my good (Romans 8:28).

I am free from any condemning charges against me because God is for me (Romans 8:31-34).

I am constantly being prayed for according to the perfect will of God by Jesus (Romans 8:34; Hebrews 7:25).

I cannot be separated from the love of God that is in Jesus (Romans 8:35-39).

I can do all things through Christ who strengthens me (Philippians 4:13).

I am significant in Christ

I am a minister of reconciliation for God (2 Corinthians 5:17-21).

I am the salt of the earth (Matthew 5:13).

I am the light of the world (Matthew 5:14).

I am chosen by God, holy and dearly loved (Colossians 3:12; 1 Thessalonians 1:4).

I am a member of Christ's Body and have a unique role to play in the Church (1 Corinthians 12:27; Ephesians 5:30).

I am seated in the heavenly places with Jesus (Ephesians 2:6).

I am a temple – a dwelling place of God. His Spirit and His life dwells in me (1 Corinthians 6:19).

I am God's co-worker (1 Corinthians 3:9; 2 Corinthians 6:1).

I have been purchased with the imperishable and precious blood of Jesus (1 Peter 1:19).

I can approach God with freedom, confidence, and boldness through Jesus (Ephesians 3:12; Hebrews 4:16).

I am a child of light, not of darkness (1 Thessalonians 5:5).

I am a member of a chosen race, a royal priesthood, a holy nation, God's special possession (1 Peter 2:9-10).

I have been chosen and appointed to bear fruit, fruit that will last (John 15:16).

I have received all of God's promises in Jesus Christ (2 Corinthians 1:20).

I am God's workmanship, created to do good works (Ephesians 2:10).

I am a partaker of God's divine nature (2 Peter 1:4).

I was chosen by God before the creation of the world (Ephesians 1:4).

I am an expression of the life of Christ because He is my life (Colossians 3:4).

I am a holy partaker in a heavenly calling (Hebrews 3:1).

I am a branch of the true vine, a channel of His life to others (John 15:1, 5).

Adapted from Rodney Hogue, "Liberated" & Neil Anderson, "Living Free in Christ"

Appendix C

Prayer of Surrender

Dear Father,

Thank You for delivering me from life in Adam and placing me in Christ Jesus.

I confess that I have been living a self-sufficient life and have been struggling to live the Christian life out of my own resources. I have realized that apart from Christ, I can do nothing, in and of myself, that brings eternal value.

I admit that I have been trying to get my needs met through people, achievements, and possessions.

I now give up on my self-sufficiency and do hereby commit my life unconditionally into Your hands. I surrender all my rights and expectations and come into agreement with You to make me into the kind of person You created me to be.

I believe Your Word that I have been crucified with Christ, am dead to sin, buried, and have been raised with Him into newness of life. I have ascended with Him into the heavenly places, and I believe that I now am seated at the right hand of the Father.

I choose as an act of my will to believe that Christ is my life, my power, and my identity. I thank You that in Christ I am totally accepted and acceptable and that all my needs are met by Him.

I yield myself totally to Christ to live His life through me. Glorify and manifest Your Son in me. I'm trusting You, in Your timing, to make this real in my experience.

I choose to believe these truths regardless of what my circumstances may be or how I feel.

In His Identity,

Appendix D

Assurance of a Saving Relationship with Christ

According to the Bible, salvation is through faith in the name of Jesus Christ. See Acts 3:16.

I believe by calling on the name of the Lord Jesus, I am saved. See Romans 10:13.

By faith, I trust the only work I have to do on this earth is to believe in Jesus according to my union with Him—Who He says He is and who He says I am. See John 6:28-29.

I believe that Jesus is the crucified, dead, buried, risen, seated Son of the living God. See Romans 6:3-6.

I believe, by faith, in the finished work of the cross. See Galatians 2:20.

I receive by faith everything for life and godliness to live life on this earth. See 2 Peter 1:3-4.

I believe that God will finish the work He has begun in me. See Philippians 1:6.

I believe that sanctification is the power of God at work in me to carry out His purposes and plan. See Ephesians 3:20.

I believe that God prepared works for me before the foundation of the world to walk in on earth. Ephesians 2:10.

I believe I am seated in the heavenlies with Christ at the right hand of God, awaiting the final judgment of unbelievers. See Ephesians 2:6.

I believe I will spend eternity with the Trinity in heaven. See John 5:24.

Appendix E

Forgiveness Assignment

What is involved in forgiving someone? Forgiveness is a decision, a choice, based on an act of the will – NOT a feeling. It is recognizing that I've been totally forgiven by God, and the debt I owe God has been canceled. ("Father, I thank You that all my sins past, present, and future were paid for by the death of Your Son, Jesus Christ, on the cross, and they will never be held against me in the future.")

1. On a separate piece of paper, make a list of all of the people in your life (that God brings to mind) who have been an offense to you, have hurt you, or sinned against you. In this exercise, you will be forgiving others and releasing yourself from past hurts and sins, and God from past hurts. Pray: Heavenly Father, please bring to my mind the people You want me to forgive and put on my forgiveness list.

    a. List the actual offense (hurt or sin) done to you by that person.

   b. List any former or present feelings towards the offender.

   c. List any judgments against the offender.

   d. List any lies about God, self, or others.

2. A common deception is to think that just because you know how to forgive someone or have thought about it (or even made the list), it is the same as actually doing it. Faith requires obedience. You actually need to sit down and forgive.

Appendix F

The Completed Works of Christ

(Very limited list)

He Has Given Us:

1. Freedom from sin's control—See Romans 6:11

2. His faith—See Galatians 2:20, TPT

3. Repentance by giving us His mind—See 1 Corinthians 2:16

4. The Fruit of the Spirit—See Galatians 5:22-23

5. Grace—See Philippians 3:10-11

6. Freedom to relinquish our rights—See Isaiah 30:18-22

7. The ability to walk in good works—See Ephesians 2:10

8. Forgiveness—See Colossians 3:12-14

9. A new identity—See 1 John 4:17c

10. Our completeness in Him—See Psalm 34:10; Psalm 84:11; Colossians 2:10

11. Life—See 2 Corinthians 5:17

12. He sanctified, glorified, transformed, and redeemed us—See Romans 3:24; Romans 8:29-30; 1 Corinthians 6:11; Corinthians 9:8, TPT and Footnote

13. Justification—See Galatians 2:16-17; Romans 5:1-2; Romans 5:8-10

14. An obedient heart—See Romans 1:5; 1 Peter 1:14; 2 Peter 1:3

15. Everything we need for life and godliness—See 2 Peter 1:3

16. Full, unconditional acceptance—See Romans 8:14-16, TPT

Appendix G

Our Union with Christ

Romans 6:3-7, TPT - Or have you forgotten that all of us who were immersed into union with Jesus, the Anointed One, were immersed into union with His death? Sharing in His death by our baptism means that we were co-buried with Him, so that when the Father's glory raised Christ from the dead, we were also raised with Him. We have been co-resurrected with Him so that we could be empowered to walk in the freshness of new life. For since we are permanently grafted into Him to experience a death like His, then we are permanently grafted into Him to experience a resurrection like His and the new life that it imparts. Could it be any clearer that our former identity is now and forever deprived of its power? For we were co-crucified with Him to dismantle the stronghold of sin within us, so that we would not continue to live one moment longer submitted to sin's power. Obviously, a dead person is incapable of sinning.

Colossians 3:1-4, TPT - Christ's resurrection is your resurrection too. This is why we are to yearn for all that is above, for that's where Christ sits enthroned at the place of all power, honor, and authority! Yes, *feast on all the treasures of the heavenly realm* and fill your thoughts with heavenly realities, and not with the distractions of the natural realm. Your crucifixion with Christ has severed the tie to this life, and now your true life is hidden away in God in Christ. And as Christ Himself is seen for who He really is, who you really are will also be revealed, for you are now one with Him in His glory!

Romans 8:9-11, TPT - But when the Spirit of Christ empowers your life, you are not dominated by the flesh but by the Spirit. And if you are not joined to the Spirit of the Anointed One, you are not of Him. Now Christ lives His life in you! And even though your body may be dead because of the effects of sin, His life-giving Spirit imparts life to you because you are fully accepted by God. Yes, God raised Jesus to life! And since God's Spirit of Resurrection lives in you, He will also raise your dying body to life by the same Spirit that breathes life into you!

2 Corinthians 5:17, TPT – Now, if anyone is enfolded into Christ, He has become an entirely new person. All that is related to the old order has vanished. Behold, everything is fresh and new.

Ephesians 1:3-6, TPT - Every spiritual blessing in the heavenly realm has already been lavished upon us as a love gift from our wonderful heavenly Father, the Father of our Lord Jesus — all because He sees us wrapped into Christ. This is why we celebrate Him with all our hearts! And in love, He chose us before He laid the foundation of the universe! Because of His great love, He ordained us so that we would be seen as holy in His eyes with an unstained innocence. For it was always in His perfect plan to adopt us as His delightful children, through our union with Jesus, the Anointed One, so that His tremendous love that cascades over us would glorify His grace —for the same love He has for the Beloved, Jesus, He has for us. And this unfolding plan brings Him great pleasure!

Philippians 3:8-10, TPT - To truly know Him meant letting go of everything from my past and throwing all my boasting on the garbage heap. It's all like a pile of manure to me now, so that I may be enriched in the reality of knowing Jesus Christ and embrace Him as Lord in all of His greatness. My passion is to be consumed with Him and not cling to my own "righteousness" based in keeping the written Law. My only "righteousness" will be His, based on the faithfulness of Jesus Christ—the very righteousness that comes from God. And I continually long to know the wonders of Jesus and to experience the overflowing power of His resurrection working in me. I will be one with

Him in His sufferings and become like Him in His death.

1 Peter 1:3-4, TPT - Celebrate with praises the God and Father of our Lord Jesus Christ, who has shown us His extravagant mercy. For His *fountain of* mercy has given us a new life—we are reborn to experience a living, energetic hope through the resurrection of Jesus Christ from the dead. We are reborn into a perfect inheritance that can never perish, never be defiled, and never diminish. It is promised and preserved forever in the heavenly realm for you!

John 14:15, TPT - "Loving Me empowers you to obey My commands."

John 17:20-23, TPT - "And I ask not only for these disciples, but also for all those who will one day believe in Me through their message. I pray for them all to be joined together as one even as you and I, Father, are joined together as one. I pray for them to become one with us so that the world will recognize that You sent Me. For the very glory You have given to Me I have given them so that they will be joined together as one and experience the same unity that we enjoy. You live fully in Me and now I live fully in them so that they will experience perfect unity, and the world will be convinced that you have sent Me, for they will see that You love each one of them with the same passionate love that you have for Me."

Romans 8:13-14, TPT - For when you live controlled by the flesh, you are about to die. But if the life of the Spirit puts to death the corrupt ways of the flesh, we then taste His abundant life. The mature children of God are those who are moved by the impulses of the Holy Spirit.

Galatians 2:20, TPT - My old identity has been co-crucified with Christ and no longer lives. And now the essence of this new life is no longer mine, for the Anointed One lives His life through me—*we live in union as one!* My new life is empowered by the faith of the Son of God who loves me so much that He gave Himself for me, *dispensing His life into mine!*

Galatians 5:5, TPT - But we have the true hope that comes from being made right with God, and by the Spirit we wait eagerly for this hope.

Ephesians 1:22-23, TPT - And He alone is the leader and source of everything needed in the church. God has put everything beneath the authority of Jesus Christ and has given Him the highest rank above all others. And now we, His church, are His body on the earth and that which fills Him who is being filled by it!

Philippians 3:12-14, TPT - I admit that I haven't yet acquired the absolute fullness that I'm pursuing, but I run with passion into His abundance so that I may reach the purpose for which Christ Jesus laid hold of me to make me

His own. I don't depend on my own strength to accomplish this; however, I do have one compelling focus: I forget all of the past as I fasten my heart to the future instead. I run straight for the divine invitation of reaching the heavenly goal and gaining the victory prize through the anointing of Jesus.

1 John 2:3-6, TPT - Here's how we can be sure that we've truly come to know God: if we keep His commands. If someone claims, "I have come to know God *by experience*," yet doesn't keep God's commands, he is a phony, and the truth finds no place in him. But the love of God will be perfected within the one who obeys God's Word. We can be sure that we've truly come to live in *intimacy with* God, not just by saying, "I am intimate with God," but by walking in the footsteps of Jesus.

1 John 4:17, TPT - By *living in God*, love has been brought to its full expression in us so that we may fearlessly face the day of judgment, because all that Jesus now is, so are we in this world.

About the Author

AFTER BECOMING A CHRISTIAN AT THE AGE of 12, Renée struggled with performance to get her needs met, even performing for God, thinking she was unacceptable to Him. In 1995, she began to understand the Truth of Galatians 2:20. Because of her co-crucifixion with Christ, she now knows she is fully loved, forgiven, and has an identity as a New Creation in Christ (2 Corinthians 5:17). She is fully accepted (and acceptable) in the Beloved because of His finished work on the cross (Romans 8:15, TPT). With a passion for teaching the truths of the New Covenant of Grace, she pursued training in counseling and instruction. In 2000, she stepped away from a 30-year music career to follow God's leading and share these truths with others. As a result, God dramatically called her out of a life she had always known, and He has become her LIFE as she embraces all that God wants to do in and through her. Her heart is to reach people with the Truth of the Gospel, that not only have we been forgiven by the shed blood of Jesus, but Christ has come into union with us and is our LIFE! He did this by giving His body for us on the Cross and crucifying us with Him, so that He could live His Life through us as us (Galatians 2:20; 1 John 4:17c).

After 27 years of marriage, Renée's husband died suddenly in 1997. God revealed a new plan and path for her. Renée comes to Abundant Grace International from almost

20 years at Grace Life International, a sister office in Charlotte, NC, where she served as Assistant Director of Counseling. She is a Discipleship Counselor, teacher, trainer, author, and conference speaker. She was born and raised in Columbia, SC, and spent her married years in Blythewood, SC. She is a proud Mama to two married children, and delights in being a Mimi to seven grandchildren and three great-grandchildren.

Suggested References

Counseling, coaching, training sites:

Network220.org – Location tab for the nearest office (many offices offer
online counseling)

Teaching websites:

The Grace Message with Dr. Andrew Farley (andrewfarley.org)
John Lynch – johnlynchspeaks.com
Ralph Harris – ralphharris.org
Frank Friedman – ourresolutehope.com
Tim Chalas – gracelifefellowship.org
Mark Maulding – Search YouTube (God's Best Kept Secret) –
mark@gracelifeinternational.com
Malcolm Smith - unconditionallovefellowship.com
Joseph Prince – josephprince.org
Bob George – bobgeorge.net
Joel Brueseke – growingingrace.org
Mike Kapler – growingingrace.org

Reading Resources:

Mark Maulding – God's Best Kept Secret
Andrew Farley – The Perfect You
Hudson Taylor – Union Communion
A B Simpson – Himself (download)